INDIANA
Macmillan/McGraw-Hill TIMELINKS

People and Places

PROGRAM AUTHORS
James A. Banks
Kevin P. Colleary
Linda Greenow
Walter C. Parker
Emily M. Schell
Dinah Zike

CONTRIBUTORS
Raymond C. Jones
Irma M. Olmedo

Macmillan/McGraw-Hill

Culture

PROGRAM AUTHORS

James A. Banks, Ph.D.
Kerry and Linda Killinger Professor
 of Diversity Studies and Director, Center
 for Multicultural Education
University of Washington
Seattle, Washington

Kevin P. Colleary, Ed.D.
Curriculum and Teaching Department
Graduate School of Education
Fordham University
New York, New York

Linda Greenow, Ph.D.
Associate Professor and Chair
Department of Geography
State University of New York at New Paltz
New Paltz, New York

Walter C. Parker, Ph.D.
Professor of Social Studies Education,
 Adjunct Professor of Political Science
University of Washington
Seattle, Washington

Emily M. Schell, Ed.D.
Visiting Professor, Teacher Education
San Diego State University
San Diego, California

Dinah Zike
Educational Consultant
Dinah-Mite Activities, Inc.
San Antonio, Texas

CONTRIBUTORS

Raymond C. Jones, Ph.D.
Director of Secondary Social Studies
 Education
Wake Forest University
Winston-Salem, North Carolina

Irma M. Olmedo
Associate Professor
University of Illinois-Chicago
College of Education
Chicago, Illinois

HISTORIANS/SCHOLARS

Jeffery D. Long, Ph.D.
Associate Professor of Religious
 and Asian Studies
Elizabethtown College
Elizabethtown, Pennsylvania

Mac Dixon-Fyle, Ph.D.
Professor of History
DePauw University
Greencastle, Indiana

Shabbir Mansuri
Founding Director
Council on Islamic Education
Fountain Valley, California

Oscar J. Martinez, Ph.D.
Regents Professor of History
University of Arizona
Tucson, Arizona

GRADE LEVEL REVIEWERS

Brigid Kemper
Second Grade Teacher
Brook Park Elementary School
Indianapolis, Indiana

Kathleen Clark
Second Grade Teacher
Edison Elementary School
Fraser, Michigan

Patricia Hinchliff
Second Grade Teacher
West Woods School
Hamden, Connecticut

Pamela South
Second Grade Teacher
Greenwood Elementary School
Princess Anne, Maryland

Karen Starr
Second Grade Teacher
Arthur Froberg Elementary School
Rockford, Illinois

EDITORIAL ADVISORY BOARD

Bradley R. Bakle
Assistant Superintendent
East Allen County Schools
New Haven, Indiana

Marilyn Barr
Assistant Superintendent for Instruction
Clyde-Savannah Central School
Clyde, New York

Lisa Bogle
Elementary Coordinator, K-5
Rutherford County Schools
Murfreesboro, Tennessee

Janice Buselt
Campus Support, Primary and ESOL
Wichita Public Schools
Wichita, Kansas

Kathy Cassioppi
Social Studies Coordinator
Rockford Public Schools, District 205
Rockford, Illinois

Denise Johnson, Ph.D.
Social Studies Supervisor
Knox County Schools
Knoxville, Tennessee

Steven Klein, Ph.D.
Social Studies Coordinator
Illinois School District U-46
Elgin, Illinois

Sondra Markman
Curriculum Director
Warren Township Board of Education
Warren Township, New Jersey

Cathy Nelson
Social Studies Coordinator
Columbus Public Schools
Columbus, Ohio

Holly Pies
Social Studies Coordinator
Vigo County Schools
Terre Haute, Indiana

Avon Ruffin
Social Studies County Supervisor
Winston-Salem/Forsyth Schools
Lewisville, North Carolina

Chuck Schierloh
Social Studies Curriculum Team Leader
Lima City Schools
Lima, Ohio

Bob Shamy
Social Studies Supervisor
East Brunswick Public Schools
East Brunswick, New Jersey

Judy Trujillo
Social Studies Coordinator
Columbia Missouri School District
Columbia, Missouri

Todd Wigginton
Coordinator of Social Studies K-12
Metropolitan Nashville Public Schools
Nashville, Tennessee

The *McGraw·Hill* Companies

Macmillan McGraw-Hill

Copyright © 2010 by The McGraw-Hill Companies, Inc. All rights reserved. Except as permitted under the United States Copyright Act, no part of this publication may be reproduced or distributed in any form or by any means, or stored in a database or retrieval system, without prior permission of the publisher.
Send all inquires to: Macmillan/McGraw-Hill, 8787 Orion Place, Columbus, OH 43240-4027

MHID 0-02-153374-1   ISBN 978-0-02-153374-9   Printed in the United States of America

1 2 3 4 5 6 7 8 9 10   058/043   13 12 11 10 09 08

People and Places

Table of Contents

Unit 1 We Live Together

How do we live together? 1

Skills and Features

Maps

Unit 1

EXPLORE The Big Idea

How do we live together?

LOG ON

Find out more about living together at www.macmillanmh.com

We Live Together

People, Places, and Events

People of Jasper

The **people of Jasper** live, work, learn, and play together.

Jasper is a city in **Indiana**.

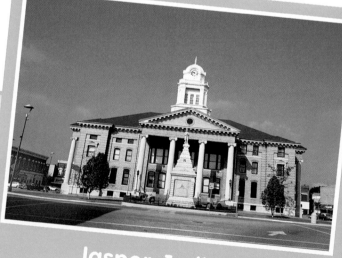

Jasper, Indiana

Strassenfest

The people of Jasper have a
special festival called **Strassenfest.**

Lesson 1

Vocabulary

guardian

time line

vote

Reading Skill

Main Idea and Details

Main Idea

Detail Detail Detail

At Home and School

We Belong to Families

Hope lives with her grandmother. Hope's grandmother is her **guardian**. A guardian takes care of you just like a parent.

Families come in many shapes and sizes. Families often live together and take care of each other. They have fun together, too!

 Who is in your family?

Family Rules

Families have rules, too. Family rules keep things fair. They help us get along together and keep us safe.

Sesha shares a room with her older sister, Pam. Sesha likes to be fair. "Pick up your toys" is a rule that Sesha follows. It makes her sister Pam happy, too!

2001

I am born.

2004

I learn to pick up my toys.

"Respect each other" is a rule that helps Sesha's family get along. "Always tell an adult where you are going" is a rule that keeps both Sesha and Pam safe.

Sesha made a **time line** of her life. It shows some of the rules that she has learned. A time line shows the order in which things happen.

 What rules do you follow at home?

2006

Pam teaches me to ride a bike.

2008

I tell an adult where I am going.

Getting Along at School

Sometimes we do not all agree. One way we get along at school is to **vote**. To vote means to make a choice about something. Mrs. Roya's class voted for a class leader. The person with the most votes won.

Just like at home, we follow rules to get along at school. "Clean up your work area" and "Raise your hand before you speak" are classroom rules that help us get along.

 On what day did Mrs. Roya's class vote?

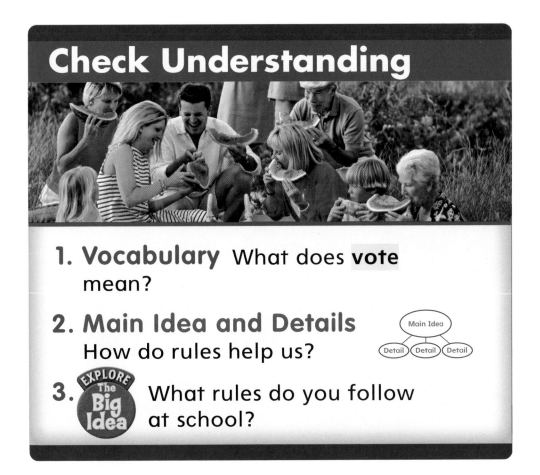

Check Understanding

1. **Vocabulary** What does **vote** mean?

2. **Main Idea and Details** How do rules help us?

   Main Idea
   Detail Detail Detail

3. **EXPLORE The Big Idea** What rules do you follow at school?

Democracy in Action

Being Honest

There are many ways to be honest. One way is to tell the truth. Another way is to not take something that does not belong to you.

Mr. Star's class collected food for hungry families. Read what happened when Bill decided to take a box of raisins.

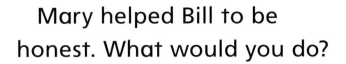

Mary helped Bill to be honest. What would you do?

There are 12 boxes of these yummy raisins. No one would miss one box.

Yes, but the raisins do not belong to us.

You are right. These raisins belong to the hungry families.

Lesson 2

Vocabulary

community

citizen

law

Reading Skill

Main Idea and Details

Main Idea

Detail   Detail   Detail

Living in Communities

What Is a Community?

A **community** is a place where people live, work, learn, and have fun together. Communities have homes, work places, schools, and places to play. They come in all shapes and sizes. Communities are made up of many neighborhoods together.

 What is a community?

Places
Indianapolis, Indiana

Indianapolis is a very large community in Indiana. There are many things to see and do in Indianapolis. These people are riding in a boat together just for fun!

Neighbors in Indianapolis

Carmen and Mrs. Tran both live in Indianapolis, Indiana. They are neighbors. Carmen helps Mrs. Tran water her garden.

Mrs. Tran helps Carmen, too. Every Tuesday Mrs. Tran drives Carmen to meet Mr. Lund at the community park. Carmen plays baseball at the park!

Mr. Lund is Carmen's baseball coach. He lives in the community of Indianapolis, too. He lives in a different neighborhood than Carmen and Mrs. Tran.

 Where do you have fun in your community?

Getting Along in a Community

A **citizen** is a person who belongs to a community. A good citizen helps others and follows community rules. Rules in a community are called **laws**. Just like rules at home and school, laws keep people safe and help them get along.

Using a leash keeps your pet safe. It is a law in many communities.

Citizens can vote for new laws. Good laws help to solve community problems. They make our community a better place to live.

 What do you think happens when people do not follow laws?

Check Understanding

1. **Vocabulary** What is a **law**?

2. **Main Idea and Details** What are communities made up of?

3. How can people in communities get along?

Map and Globe Skills

Use Grid Maps

A **grid map** is a map that is divided into squares. A letter and a number give the name for each square. The letters are on the sides of the map. The numbers are on the top and bottom.

Look at the grid map of a community on the next page. Put your finger on the first square in the top row. The square is A1. The school is in square A1.

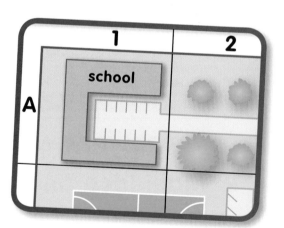

Community Grid Map

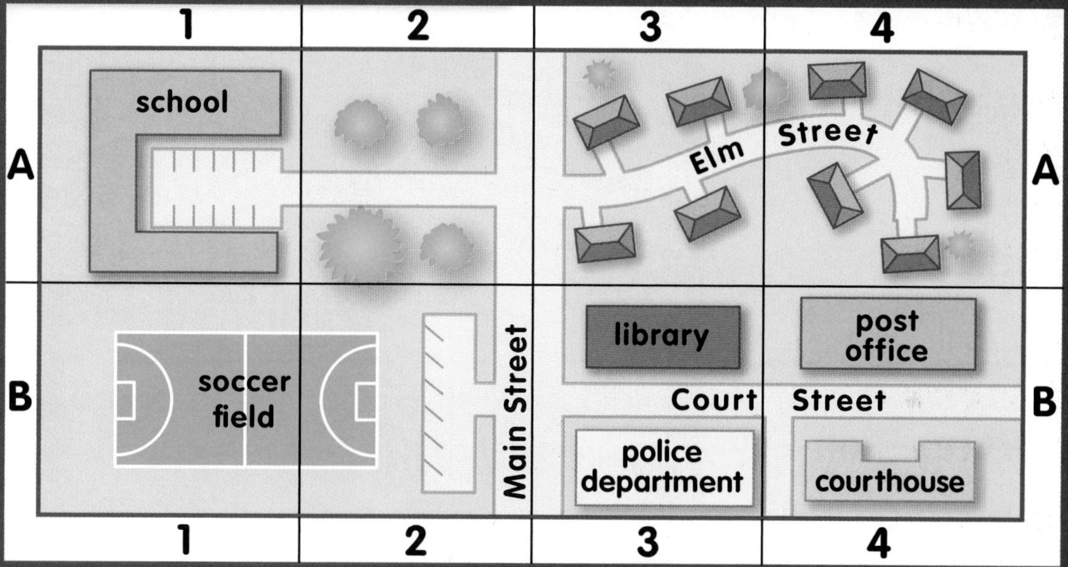
1
2
3
4
A
B
school
Elm
Street
library
post office
soccer field
Main Street
Court
Street
police department
courthouse

Try the Skill

1. What is a **grid map**?
2. Find the library. Which square is it in on the grid map?

Writing Activity

Make a grid map of your classroom, school, or community. Write labels to show what is on the map.

Communities Large and Small

Lesson 3

Vocabulary

urban

suburban

rural

Reading Skill

Main Idea and Details

Main Idea

Detail   Detail   Detail

Urban Communities

There are three kinds of communities. A city, like Indianapolis, is an **urban** community. Urban communities have many tall stores and buildings. The streets and sidewalks are busy with people, cars, buses, and taxis.

 What is an urban community?

Around the World

Hanoi is an urban community in Vietnam. In Hanoi many people use bicycles and motorbikes to move from place to place.

Two Communities

New York City is a very large urban community. Joey and Mark live there. They walk to school with their mother.

Joey and Mark's mother rides a special train, called a subway, to work. There are many ways to go from place to place in an urban community like New York.

taxi

subway

Cindy and her sisters live in a house in Freeport. Freeport is close to New York City. A community near a city is called a **suburban** community.

Suburban communities are less crowded than urban communities. There are not as many places to work. Cindy's parents travel to New York City for their jobs.

 What is a suburban community?

Rural Communities

Hazel lives on a farm in Paines Hollow, New York. Paines Hollow is a **rural** community. Rural communities are far from cities. They have lots of open land.

Hazel rides a school bus to get to school. From Paines Hollow it takes a long time to get to schools or stores.

Hazel helps raise chickens on the farm. She will bring her best chicken to the New York State Fair this summer. Last year, Hazel won a red ribbon.

 What is a rural community?

Check Understanding

1. **Vocabulary** Is your community **urban**, **suburban**, or **rural**?

2. **Main Idea and Details** What might you find in a suburban community?

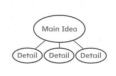

Main Idea
Detail Detail Detail

3. **EXPLORE The Big Idea** How is rural life different from urban life?

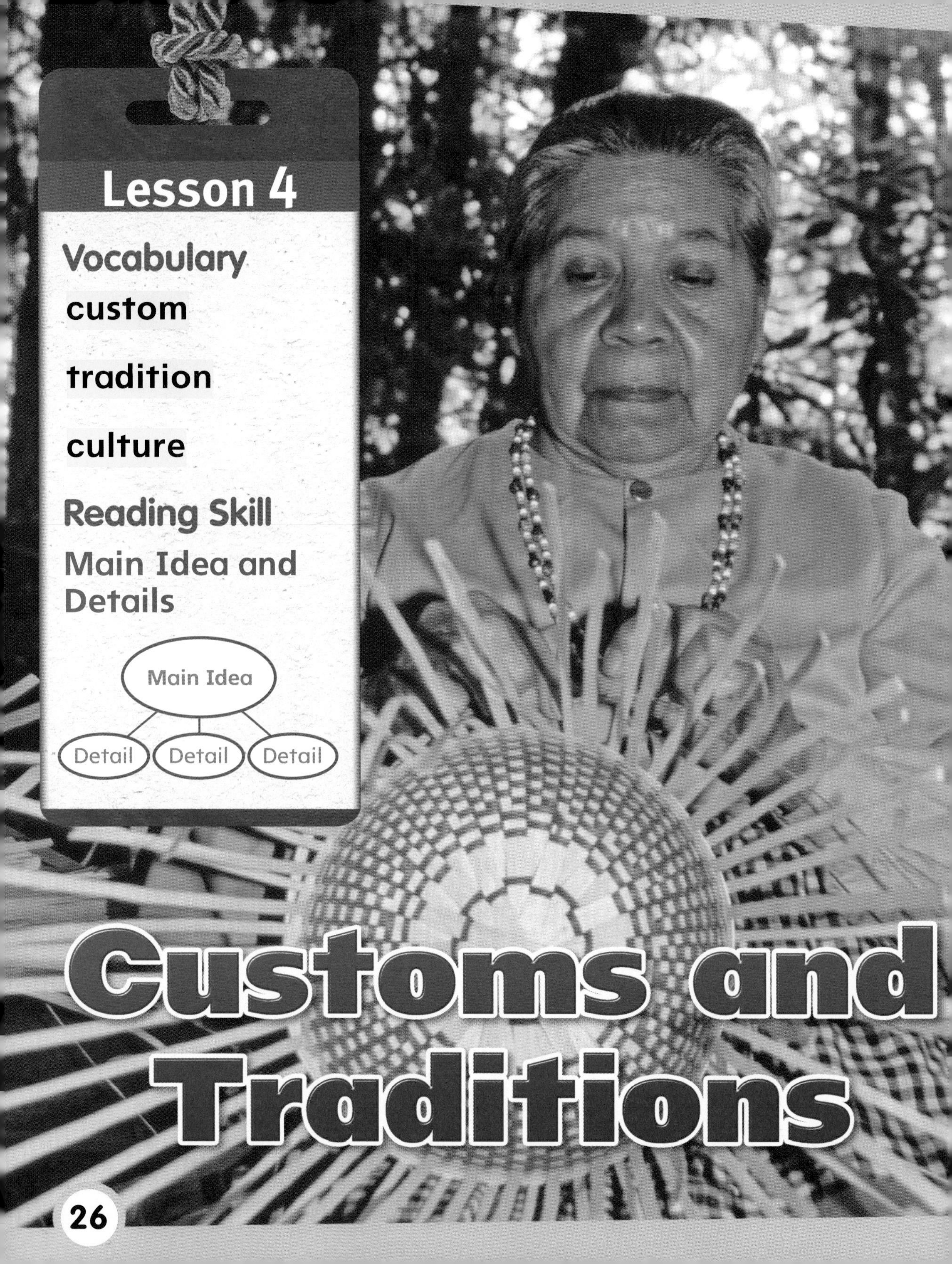

Lesson 4

Vocabulary

custom

tradition

culture

Reading Skill

Main Idea and Details

Main Idea

Detail | Detail | Detail

Customs and Traditions

Customs

A **custom** is a special way of doing something. Many families celebrate birthdays with a cake. Some Native American groups make baskets with special designs.

Communities can have customs, too. Some communities have festivals or fairs to celebrate things that make them special.

 What customs do you know?

Event
Nut Club Festival

Evansville, Indiana has a custom. Each fall they celebrate the West Side Nut Club Festival with food, parades, and rides. Don't miss the hunt for the nut contest!

Traditions

A **tradition** is a custom that is passed down over time. Hatim's uncle learned to make pita sandwiches when he lived in Libya. Today, he shows Hatim how to make them.

When Hatim grows up, he will teach his children to make pita sandwiches, too. Making pita sandwiches is a tradition in Hatim's family.

Mrs. Etana's family is from a small village in West Africa. She likes to tell stories about her village. Mrs. Etana says the tradition of telling stories was started long ago by *griots*. A griot is a person who learns stories by memory and tells them to others.

 What traditions do you know?

Sharing Culture

Culture is the way a group of people live, including their music, customs, and traditions. We can share our culture with one another.

Juan and his father play the guitar. They play a kind of Mexican music called *mariachi*. Juan and his father will share their Mexican culture at the Cincy-Cinco festival in Cincinnati, Ohio.

Lisa knows how to eat her food with chopsticks. In the culture of China, people use chopsticks. All of our cultures together make up the culture of the United States.

 What comes from the culture of China?

Check Understanding

1. **Vocabulary** What is **culture**?

2. **Main Idea and Details** What do you know about customs?

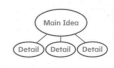

3. How do different cultures make our communities special?

Lesson 5

Vocabulary

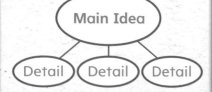

inventor

scientist

Reading Skill

Main Idea and Details

Main Idea

Detail   Detail   Detail

People Help Communities

Artists

Artists are people who make art. Some artists paint, sing, or dance. Others build beautiful things. Artists make our communities better places to live.

Alicia Keys sings and plays the piano. She started playing piano when she was only seven years old. Today her music brings joy to people in many communities.

 How do artists make a difference?

People
Maya Lin

Maya Lin created this skating rink in Grand Rapids, Michigan. She said, "I try to give people a different way of looking at their surroundings. . . . That's art to me."

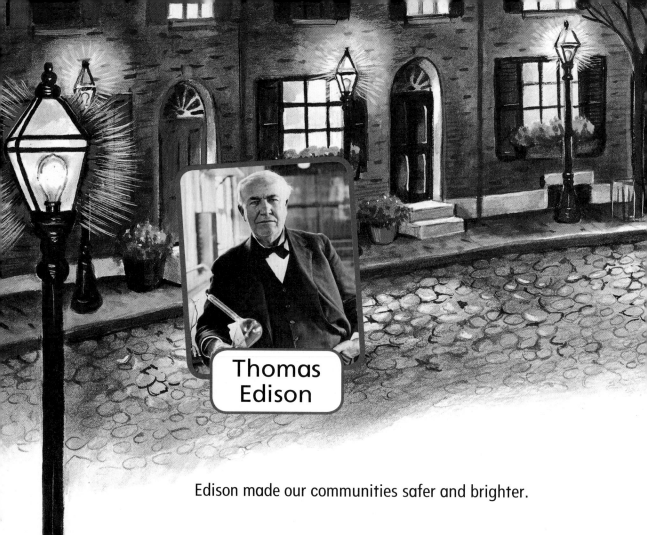

Thomas Edison

Edison made our communities safer and brighter.

Inventors and Scientists

Thomas Edison was an **inventor**. An inventor is a person who makes something for the first time. Edison made a light bulb that could shine a long time. He also invented a way to record sound.

Mae Jemison studies space. She is a **scientist**. A scientist is a person who works to understand and explain nature. Jemison was the first African American woman to fly in space! She runs a space camp for children aged 12 to 16.

Mae Jemison

 What does an inventor do?

Check Understanding

1. **Vocabulary** What is a **scientist**?

2. **Main Idea and Details** How do inventors help us?

 3. Who are some people who have helped your community?

Review and Assess

Vocabulary

Number a paper from 1 to 3. Next to each number write the word that matches the meaning.

guardian   **citizen**   **inventor**

1. a person who makes something for the first time

2. a person who takes care of you like a parent

3. a person who belongs to a community

Critical Thinking

4. Why is voting important?

5. How did Thomas Edison help our communities?

Use Grid Maps

Look at the grid map below. Then answer the question.

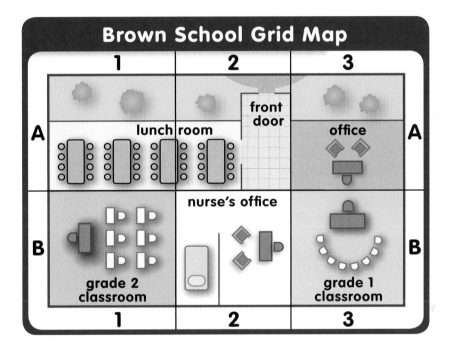

Brown School Grid Map

6. Which room is in square B3?

    A. nurse's office

    B. grade I classroom

    C. lunch room

    D. grade 2 classroom

Community Activity

Make a Community Book

1. On three pages, draw I.) where you live, 2.) where you learn, and 3.) a place where you have fun.

2. Write what is in each picture.

3. Make a cover. Staple the pages and the cover together to make a book.

4. Share your book with your class.

I live in a big building.

I play at the park.

Picture Glossary

C

citizen A person who belongs to a community. *A good citizen helps others in his or her community.* (page 16)

community A place where people live, work, learn, and have fun together. *I live in the community of Ouray, Colorado.* (page 13)

culture The way a group of people live, including their music, customs, and traditions. *Using chopsticks is from the culture of China.* (page 30)

custom A special way of doing something. *Traverse City, Michigan, has a custom of celebrating cherries every July.* (page 27)

G

grid map A map that is divided into squares. *The post office is located in square B4 on the grid map.* (page 19)

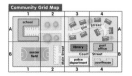

guardian A person who takes care of you like a parent. *Hope's guardian helps her plant flowers in their yard.* (page 5)

I

inventor A person who makes something for the first time. *Thomas Edison was the inventor of the lightbulb.* (page 34)

L

law A rule in a community. *In many communities, it is a law to keep a dog on a leash.* (page 16)

R

rural An area that is far away from a city. *My dad's horse farm is in a rural community.* (page 24)

S

scientist A person who works to understand and explain nature. *Mae Jemison is a scientist who studies space.* (page 35)

suburban An area that is near a city. *Cindy and her sisters live in a suburban community.* (page 23)

T

time line A line that shows the order in which things happen. *This is a time line of Sesha's life.* (page 7)

tradition A custom that is passed down over time. *Learning to play mariachi is a **tradition** in Luke's family.* (page 28)

urban The area of a city. *New York City is an **urban** community.* (page 21)

vote To make a choice about something. *The class held a **vote** to choose a class leader.* (page 8)

Index

This index lists many things you can find in your book. It tells the page numbers on which they are found. If you see the letter *m* before a page number, you will find a map on that page.

Credits